I0067330

# BOLD
## Questions

52 questions
to shape how you
make decisions

# Jill J. Johnson, MBA

Johnson
Consulting
Services
*Marketing & Management Consultants*

Other books by Jill J. Johnson:

From the BOLD Questions Series

BOLD Questions – Business Strategy Edition
BOLD Questions – Opportunities Edition
BOLD Questions – Leadership Edition


Learn more about Jill online and check out her free white papers at:

www.jcs-usa.com

DECISION-MAKING EDITION

# BOLD
## Questions

### 52 questions
to shape how you
make decisions

## Jill J. Johnson, MBA

Johnson
Consulting
Services
Marketing & Management Consultants

BOLD Questions – Decision-Making Edition

Published by Johnson Consulting Services
Minneapolis, Minnesota
www.jcs-usa.com

Book Design by Chris Mendoza

For information on Jill or on how to order bulk copies of this book, or the BOLD Questions series, contact her at:
www.jcs-usa.com

ISBN: 978-0-9984236-3-0

Printed in the United States of America

**This book is dedicated to my clients.**

You have inspired me and taught me so much about how to develop impactful strategies, take advantage of opportunities, lead effectively and make difficult decisions.

# ABOUT JILL

An award-winning management consultant, Jill J. Johnson has personally impacted $4 billion worth of business decisions through her consulting work. She is in the board rooms, the back rooms and the executive suites where complex decisions are being made, impacting the future of clients located throughout the United States, as well as in Europe and Asia. She knows what it takes to develop and implement strategies for turnarounds or growth that get results.

Jill is a widely-respected business executive and leader who has been a member of the boards of directors and executive committees of a variety of business, professional and governmental boards. She has served on two federal boards under three different United States presidents representing both political parties.

Jill has won numerous honors for her business acumen, her leadership savvy, mentorship skills and her entrepreneurial successes. Jill is also one of the first women ever inducted into both the Minnesota Women Business Owners Hall of Fame and the Top Women in Finance Hall of Fame.

Over the years, Jill has been quoted on a range of management issues in national publications including *The Wall Street Journal, The New York Times, Inc., Money Magazine* and *Entrepreneur.* She has appeared as a thought leader on a variety of radio and television programs for business. She is a 4th generation entrepreneur who grew up in a family-owned business.

Jill is a powerful speaker with the rare ability to deliver substantive content in a way that is engaging and easily accessible. She is also a Professional Member of the National Speakers Association.

Jill resides in Minneapolis, Minnesota.

Talk to Jill about how her Consulting Services can help you gain the clarity you need to develop your business strategies. Book Jill to Speak at your next event. Contact her at:

> www.jcs-usa.com
> www.twitter.com/JillJohnsonUSA
> www.facebook.com/JohnsonConsultingServices
> www.linkedin.com/in/JohnsonConsultingServices

# ACKNOWLEDGMENTS

Thank you to everyone who encouraged me to share this book series with the world. You have made this book possible.

**To my family:**
To my husband, Jack Tebbe. Thank you so much for your endless support of me and for always believing in my dreams.

To my sister, Jaci Johnson. Your insight and feedback have always been extraordinarily valuable to me.

**To my book team:**
Isabella Dotzler for sharing your editing skills and ideas as I pieced together the detailed concepts for this book series.

Lorelei Kraft for encouraging me to move forward with writing a book.

Kristen Brown for guiding me on making this book series concept tangible.

Maddi Meierotto for your assistance in helping me think through the power of quotes.

Amy Mathews for helping me finally see the possibilities for this book series.

Rachel Benrud for keeping me on track to finally getting this done.

Chris Mendoza for the cover design and formatting to turn my idea into a reality.

**To my valued insight team:**
To the 5 generations of colleagues and friends who took time out of their busy days to review these books and provide me with valuable feedback to narrow the focus down to the most critical questions. Your responses and comments proved these concepts transcend generational divides.

Bob Baynton, Patty DeDominic, Isabella Dotzler, Mary Frantz, Sharon Gifford, Maddy Gildersleeve, Sharon Horne, Katherine Hunt, Joan Kennedy, Susan McCloskey, Maddi Meierotto, Anne Neu, Kim Utecht Payfrock and Melissa Sauser.

# INTRODUCTION

Each day leaders try to bring their best efforts to their work. Yet many are overwhelmed by the complexities of today's constantly changing and unpredictable economic environment. They struggle to find focus to set the strategies they need to lead their enterprises and move their organizations forward.

Our economic, political and social environment is exceptionally volatile, uncertain, complex and ambiguous. As a result, it has become increasingly difficult to develop strategies for success when every time you turn around there is another challenge that threatens your enterprise survival. You have to navigate the challenge of leading a diverse workforce with teams comprised of different generations and widely varied understanding of the strategic roadblocks ahead. To lead in this environment, you need more from yourself and your team.

As a management consultant for more than 20 years, the executives, business owners and board of directors I work with struggle deeply with these issues. In my experience, those leaders who are open to reflection are often the most successful, the most effective, and achieve the greatest results. They are also the most confident in their leadership because they know they have considered every possible aspect of their strategies, opportunities and decisions.

Leaders who are willing to shift their mindset from their current status quo thinking will typically execute business strategies that achieve a higher level of accomplishment. Those who take the time to reflect on their options for responding to evolving market opportunities before they are in chaos have more insight and develop confident strategies to respond and take advantage of unforeseen circumstances. They also find new meaning in their roles and their own potential for business achievement.

Leaders who diligently develop their abilities and continually refine their decision making skills are more effective than their peers. They are more confident in executing strategies and decisions because they have reflected deeply on the available options and understand the consequences of their actions or inaction. They have fully considered their opportunities and are more prepared to adjust their assumptions to the evolving challenges they face.

Leaders who involve their teams in candidly discussing critical issues gain enhanced commitment to achieving enterprise goals and better buy-in when they need them to change. This is because they all understand the stakes and have a clear understanding of the issues they need to address. They are not content to wait to have strategic discussions only at an annual planning meeting. By seeding strategic issues into on-going conversations throughout the year, these leaders know they are not only building the critical thinking skills of their team members, but also providing them with the understanding of the challenges so they can bring their best ideas and innovations forward throughout the year.

Over the years, these insights have evolved into what I use as the framework for my approach to consulting. I call it the BOLD Approach. The BOLD Approach is the foundation of my management consulting practice. Regardless of the setting, this approach has provided my clients with the leadership insights they need to address critical issues threatening their survival and on-going ability to compete. This approach works in the executive suites of corporations, in entrepreneurial environments, in non-profit enterprises and in trade associations.

I have found this is one of the most effective methods you can employ to lead in an unstable business climate. It is a four-point framework to focus your strategic mindset on gaining the insight and critical skills you need to thrive. The Bold Approach is designed to impact your critical situations, influence outcomes and help you achieve greater results.

The components of the BOLD Approach focus on four key areas of review:

- Business Strategies - Grow your organization with purpose and prosperity
- Opportunities - Uncover the maximum potential in your market
- Leadership - Lead with confidence and impact
- Decision Making – Gain clarity to minimize indecision and uncertainty

My clients are success-oriented and ambitious leaders just like you. They share my passion for results and are prepared to act boldly to attain them. They want to understand the critical market forces shaping the future of their enterprises. They seek candor and are not afraid of adapting their strategic thinking to respond to evolving market and competitive dynamics.

Like you, my clients are always searching for insight and information. But knowing the critical questions to ask requires more than desire; it requires a deep focus on asking the right questions. This is why I developed the BOLD Questions Series for you.

# GETTING STARTED

Each book in the BOLD Questions Series is designed to guide you through reflection on a key element of the BOLD Approach. They are all carefully constructed to be a tool to guide your thinking and help you better focus on the most critical issues you face.

The BOLD Questions Series is designed to help you obtain the information and insight needed to achieve success. The drive toward success requires diligent action and taking time for reflection.

The quotes and issues you will find in this four volume series reflect the critical issues and key questions I ask my management consulting clients as I help them develop their strategic plans, create their strategies to maximize their growth, or resolve a turn-around situation. By addressing these questions, it will be like having me on-site with you as your personal consultant challenging your thinking and working with you to enhance your strategic mindset. The best way to use this series is to pick one key area you want to focus on and then begin.

Each book in this series hones in on 52 issues and questions you must consider. First you read the quote. Then I ask you to reflect on one or more critical questions relating to the quote. But reflection is not enough. You are then challenged to identify the actions you will take to address the question to resolve the issues or move to the next step toward your success.

Some quotes will resonate with you more deeply than others. For those quotes and questions you initially want to disregard, take a pause. Each topic was chosen because in my experience these are the difficult issues most leaders face.

When you find a question you want to skip over or only answer superficially, it is vital to recognize this is actually an area you need to focus on with even more reflection and thought! If you think you should dismiss it, you must take more time with it. This is a focus area you do not yet have enough insight to understand how important it is to your success.

# HOW TO USE THESE BOOKS

There are two different ways you can use the BOLD Questions Series:

**On Your Own** – You can use these books as a guide for your own reflections on these topic areas. Pick one book in the series as your initial focus area. Each week select a quote to reflect on. Spend at least 15 minutes reviewing the quote and reflecting on the critical question found on the opposite page. Jot down your thoughts, ideas, concerns, next steps, etc. in the space available under the question. Then decide what you are going to do about it. Use the section called Actions I Will Take to summarize what you will accomplish on this issue in the next week.

**With Your Team** – These books are also ideal for leaders who want to guide their team in a more focused way and begin a dialog about the issues that matter most to future enterprise success. Start by selecting a book in the series for your team to focus on for the next year. On a weekly basis, assign a quote to the group. Have everyone in the group individually work through the quote and question as described above. They should make notes in their own copy of the book. Then guide your team through a focused discussion of the issue and their thoughts about it. Capture all of their ideas on a sheet of paper or on the complimentary "Actions We Will Take Summary Sheet" available on my website, www.jcs-usa.com. Facilitate their discussion as they bring forward different points of view. Identify the top three actions the group comes up with that will most impact your situation. Then designate responsibility for taking action on these items during the next week to individual members of your team. When your group comes back together the following week, begin the meeting with an update on their progress. When you are done with that update, move on to focus your discussion on the next quote. Use a new copy of the "Actions We Will Take Summary Sheet" each week. By the end of the year, you and your team will have engaged in a deep dive into the most critical issues you face. Your team will be accustomed to thinking more strategically, acting as more effective leaders, making better decisions and achieving results designed to create lasting success for your enterprise.

Once you or your team are done with this book, pick up another one of the books found in this BOLD Questions Series and begin again. This will keep your thoughts and discussions moving forward and focused on the issues that really impact your potential for success.

# USING THE **BOLD** QUESTIONS SERIES

By using the entire BOLD Questions Series, you will build success on a viable future that is grounded in a realistic understanding of your situation, not wishful thinking. You will integrate an action plan for uncertainty into every facet of your strategy development.

By engaging in the disciplined focus of consistently asking the right questions to shape your leadership actions, decisions and strategies, you will sharpen the critical thinking skills necessary to thrive in today's complex business climate.

By considering the challenging questions found in all four of these books, you will have a deeper understanding of your current and evolving situation. You will build your confidence because you are developing business strategies to enhance your success. You will uncover the potential in your markets. You will become a more confident and effective leader. You will make better decisions, and so will your team.

Regardless of where you are at today in your own leadership development, by using the BOLD Questions Series you will become more influential, more impactful, and you will think with a more strategic mindset.

Wishing you much success!

Jill J. Johnson, MBA, President & Founder
Johnson Consulting Services

# P.S. Share your progress with me. You can reach me via the following:

Email: Jill@jcs-usa.com

Twitter: @JillJohnsonUSA
LinkedIn: www.linkedin.com/in/JohnsonConsultingServices
Facebook: www.facebook.com/JohnsonConsultingServices

For bulk orders, contact my office
for more information at 763-571-3101.

Access your free download of the
*"Actions We Will Take Summary Sheet"* at:
www.jcs-usa.com/ActionsWeWillTakeSummarySheet

# DECISION-MAKING EDITION

Effective decision making in an uncertain and unstable world begins with a desire for clarity. Gaining clarity requires a complete and candid understanding of your situation. Truth gives you information. Well-researched information gives you insight. Insight gives you the clarity needed to set the right priorities and focus your team on the most critical activities affecting success.

Make sure you are not operating under a false set of assumptions that were correct at one time, but have not been updated to reflect your current situation. If your assumptions are wrong, your ability to make good decisions will be severely limited by your skewed viewpoint.

It is critical that you reassess your assumptions about the future. Getting the right information for effective decision-making is essential. Look for more than superficial answers to the critical issues you face. Be willing to invest the time and money to bring in a fresh and different point of view to discover the truth.

Are you ready to ask the questions to gain the clarity you need to thrive? Let's begin.

**“**Even a non-decision is a decision.**”**

Jill J. Johnson

# Why are you hesitating with your decision?

_____

_____

_____

_____

_____

_____

_____

_____

_____

_____

_____

_____

_____

## Actions I Will Take:

_____

_____

_____

_____

_____

**"**Numerous market forces
will influence your strategic
decision making.**"**

Jill J. Johnson

# What changing market forces will influence your decisions?

_____

_____

_____

_____

_____

_____

_____

_____

_____

_____

_____

_____

_____

_____

_____

## Actions I Will Take:

_____

_____

_____

_____

_____

**"**Leaders who impact over the long-term have substance to their thoughts, actions and decisions.**"**

Jill J. Johnson

# Where is your substance?

_____
_____
_____
_____
_____
_____
_____
_____
_____
_____
_____
_____
_____
_____

# Actions I Will Take:

_____
_____
_____
_____
_____

**"**Decision making is just like any
other skill. It takes practice to
learn to do it well.**"**

*Jill J. Johnson*

# What can you work on next to make better decisions?

_____

_____

_____

_____

_____

_____

_____

_____

_____

_____

_____

_____

_____

## Actions I Will Take:

_____

_____

_____

_____

**"Beware of the frauds who masquerade as experts. They can do enormous damage."**

*Jill J. Johnson*

# Who are your advisors? Why are they the best for you?

_____

_____

_____

_____

_____

_____

_____

_____

_____

_____

_____

_____

_____

_____

_____

# Actions I Will Take:

_____

_____

_____

_____

_____

66Exceptional leaders always
rethink the key assumptions
impacting their operating, financial
and strategic planning efforts.99

*Jill J. Johnson*

# What impact will your assumptions have on your planning efforts?

_____

_____

_____

_____

_____

_____

_____

_____

_____

_____

_____

_____

_____

_____

## Actions I Will Take:

_____

_____

_____

_____

**66**When we are under enormous
*stress, we default to how our families
taught us to make decisions.***99**

Jill J. Johnson

# How did your family teach you to make decisions?

_____

_____

_____

_____

_____

_____

_____

_____

_____

_____

_____

_____

_____

## Actions I Will Take:

_____

_____

_____

_____

**"**Information provides you with the objective insight you need to make more effective decisions.**"**

Jill J. Johnson

# What objective information do you need for your decisions?

_____

_____

_____

_____

_____

_____

_____

_____

_____

_____

_____

_____

_____

_____

_____

_____

## Actions I Will Take:

_____

_____

_____

_____

_____

**"Leaders who make decisions based off emotional considerations will find it much more difficult to survive in an era of complexity."**

Jill J. Johnson

# How do you minimize the potential for making an emotional decision?

_____

_____

_____

_____

_____

_____

_____

_____

_____

_____

_____

_____

_____

_____

_____

# Actions I Will Take:

_____

_____

_____

_____

**"**The most effective leaders are those who acknowledge errors or market challenges. Then they make adjustments and move forward with a new decision.**"**

Jill J. Johnson

# What issues should you acknowledge and deal with right now?

_____

_____

_____

_____

_____

_____

_____

_____

_____

_____

_____

_____

_____

_____

_____

_____

# Actions I Will Take:

_____

_____

_____

_____

"Few decisions really require an immediate decision. You can usually take at least 24 hours to make a critical decision."

*Jill J. Johnson*

# What do you need to do to take a little time to make this decision?

_____

_____

_____

_____

_____

_____

_____

_____

_____

_____

_____

_____

_____

_____

_____

## Actions I Will Take:

_____

_____

_____

_____

**"Effective decision makers try to understand the impact of each facet of the decision at hand."**

*Jill J. Johnson*

# What are the potential impacts of your decision?

_____

_____

_____

_____

_____

_____

_____

_____

_____

_____

_____

_____

_____

# Actions I Will Take:

_____

_____

_____

_____

**"Smart leaders take calculated risks. They manage the downside as much as they do the opportunity."**

*Jill J. Johnson*

What risks do you better need to manage? How will you do this?

_____

_____

_____

_____

_____

_____

_____

_____

_____

_____

_____

_____

_____

_____

_____

## Actions I Will Take:

_____

_____

_____

_____

66Your fear may be out of proportion
to the real situation you are facing.
Maintain your perspective when you
are making a critical decision.99

*Jill J. Johnson*

# How can you gain a better perspective on your situation?

_____

_____

_____

_____

_____

_____

_____

_____

_____

_____

_____

_____

_____

_____

_____

## Actions I Will Take:

_____

_____

_____

_____

_____

**66**Your ability to reassess your
assumptions about the future
will determine your ability to
survive and thrive. **99**

*Jill J. Johnson*

# How will you reassess your assumptions?

_____

_____

_____

_____

_____

_____

_____

_____

_____

_____

_____

_____

_____

_____

_____

# Actions I Will Take:

_____

_____

_____

_____

_____

**"Even exceptionally talented leaders get paralyzed at times when facing critical decisions."**

*Jill J. Johnson*

# What do you need to face to make the decision?

_____

_____

_____

_____

_____

_____

_____

_____

_____

_____

_____

_____

_____

_____

_____

# Actions I Will Take:

_____

_____

_____

_____

**"Don't be afraid to make a bold decision."**

Jill J. Johnson

# What bold decision do you need to make? Why are you hesitating to make it?

_____

_____

_____

_____

_____

_____

_____

_____

_____

_____

_____

_____

_____

_____

_____

## Actions I Will Take:

_____

_____

_____

_____

_____

**66**When trying to solve a problem,
make sure you are looking
objectively at the situation.
You will resolve it faster.**99**

*Jill J. Johnson*

# What do you need to look at more realistically and objectively?

_____

_____

_____

_____

_____

_____

_____

_____

_____

_____

_____

_____

_____

_____

## Actions I Will Take:

_____

_____

_____

_____

_____

**❝Look for options. Look for information. Look for insight that will challenge you to think differently about your decision options.❞**

Jill J. Johnson

# Where can you find information and insight to challenge your thinking about your options?

_____

_____

_____

_____

_____

_____

_____

_____

_____

_____

_____

_____

_____

_____

## Actions I Will Take:

_____

_____

_____

_____

*66 Take action on your decisions.*
*It is not enough to just talk*
*about it. Make it happen! 99*

*Jill J. Johnson*

# What can you do right now to implement your decision?

_____

_____

_____

_____

_____

_____

_____

_____

_____

_____

_____

_____

_____

_____

# Actions I Will Take:

_____

_____

_____

_____

_____

66Effective leaders adapt to
their evolving situations.99

*Jill J. Johnson*

# What decisions do you need to make in order to respond to the changes you face?

_____
_____
_____
_____
_____
_____
_____
_____
_____
_____
_____
_____
_____

## Actions I Will Take:

_____
_____
_____
_____

**"**Use objective decision criteria
to move groups though complex
decisions. It keeps everyone focused
on the important things.**"**

Jill J. Johnson

# What objective criteria should you use to make your decision?

_____

_____

_____

_____

_____

_____

_____

_____

_____

_____

_____

_____

_____

# Actions I Will Take:

_____

_____

_____

_____

**"Make the best decision you can given the information, resources, and capabilities you have available. You can adjust your plan as necessary."**

*Jill J. Johnson*

# What is the best decision you can make right now?

_____

_____

_____

_____

_____

_____

_____

_____

_____

_____

_____

_____

_____

## Actions I Will Take:

_____

_____

_____

_____

**"Your emotions deeply influence your decisions."**

*Jill J. Johnson*

# How can you minimize emotions in your decision-making?

_____

_____

_____

_____

_____

_____

_____

_____

_____

_____

_____

_____

_____

_____

## Actions I Will Take:

_____

_____

_____

_____

66Clarity means seeing things as
they really are and understanding
what you need to do to change
the course of events.99

*Jill J. Johnson*

What do you need to see and do to change the
outcome of your situation?

_____

_____

_____

_____

_____

_____

_____

_____

_____

_____

_____

_____

_____

_____

Actions I Will Take:

_____

_____

_____

_____

66Some people easily assess all
angles of a decision while others
freeze with indecision. The critical
difference between the two is
the ability to get clarity.99

*Jill J. Johnson*

# How can you get better clarity?

_____

_____

_____

_____

_____

_____

_____

_____

_____

_____

_____

_____

_____

_____

# Actions I Will Take:

_____

_____

_____

_____

_____

**66**The best advisors are the ones
that challenge your status quo
and challenge your thinking.**99**

Jill J. Johnson

# Who are the internal and external advisors who challenge your thinking about your decisions?

_____

_____

_____

_____

_____

_____

_____

_____

_____

_____

_____

_____

_____

_____

## Actions I Will Take:

_____

_____

_____

_____

**66**When you get stuck trying to make
a big decision, break it down into
a series of smaller decisions.**99**

*Jill J. Johnson*

# What are the smaller decisions you can make right now?

_____

_____

_____

_____

_____

_____

_____

_____

_____

_____

_____

_____

_____

# Actions I Will Take:

_____

_____

_____

_____

_____

> **"**It is not enough to have a title
> or a leadership role. You must
> influence decisions or outcomes
> in order to be a real leader.**"**

Jill J. Johnson

# How can you influence the decisions being made?

_____
_____
_____
_____
_____
_____
_____
_____
_____
_____
_____
_____
_____

## Actions I Will Take:

_____
_____
_____
_____

**"When making a decision, focus on what matters - not peripheral issues."**

*Jill J. Johnson*

# What do you really need to focus on to make the best decision?

_____

_____

_____

_____

_____

_____

_____

_____

_____

_____

_____

_____

_____

_____

## Actions I Will Take:

_____

_____

_____

_____

**"**One of the most valuable skills to have as a decision maker is learning how to manage your emotions.**"**

Jill J. Johnson

# How can you become more objective in your decision making?

_____

_____

_____

_____

_____

_____

_____

_____

_____

_____

_____

_____

_____

_____

_____

## Actions I Will Take:

_____

_____

_____

_____

**"**If your goal is business survival, sometimes you need to make the hard choices and then make the decision to implement them.**"**

*Jill J. Johnson*

# How can you prepare to make the hard decision?

_____

_____

_____

_____

_____

_____

_____

_____

_____

_____

_____

_____

_____

_____

## Actions I Will Take:

_____

_____

_____

_____

_____

**66**The key to clarity is to see *things as they really are, not as you wish them to be.***99*

*Jill J. Johnson*

# What do you need to see and think about more clearly?

_____

_____

_____

_____

_____

_____

_____

_____

_____

_____

_____

_____

## Actions I Will Take:

_____

_____

_____

_____

**66**Those who reach too high
before their cash, talent, or
operational capability are ready
for that higher level of success,
risk losing everything.**99**

Jill J. Johnson

# What do you need to learn to achieve greater success?

_____

_____

_____

_____

_____

_____

_____

_____

_____

_____

_____

_____

_____

_____

_____

_____

# Actions I Will Take:

_____

_____

_____

_____

_____

**66**Don't make the consequences
of your decisions scarier
than they need to be.**99**

*Jill J. Johnson*

Can you live with the worst case consequences?
Why or why not?

_____

_____

_____

_____

_____

_____

_____

_____

_____

_____

_____

_____

_____

Actions I Will Take:

_____

_____

_____

_____

_____

**"Real market insight must flow into all aspects of your decisions."**

*Jill J. Johnson*

# What market insight should impact your decision making?

---
---
---
---
---
---
---
---
---
---
---
---
---

## Actions I Will Take:

---
---
---
---

**"**It's okay to be wrong. Everybody's wrong at some point. It's just not okay to stay wrong. So decide to adjust and make things right.**"**

Jill J. Johnson

What decision is it time for you to make?
What do you need to be ready to make it?

_____

_____

_____

_____

_____

_____

_____

_____

_____

_____

_____

_____

_____

_____

Actions I Will Take:

_____

_____

_____

_____

**"**A lack of experience limits your ability to identify decision options. Seasoned advisors have seen your situation countless times. Use their expertise.**"**

*Jill J. Johnson*

# Who are the advisors who can help you see all your options?

_____

_____

_____

_____

_____

_____

_____

_____

_____

_____

_____

_____

# Actions I Will Take:

_____

_____

_____

_____

_____

**"**Do a 360-degree review to look at your decision from every angle.**"**

Jill J. Johnson

# How can you look differently at your decision?

_____

_____

_____

_____

_____

_____

_____

_____

_____

_____

_____

_____

_____

_____

_____

_____

## Actions I Will Take:

_____

_____

_____

_____

**"Effective planning in turbulent times requires a deep assessment of the market forces influencing your business environment."**

Jill J. Johnson

# What changing market forces will influence your strategies?

_____

_____

_____

_____

_____

_____

_____

_____

_____

_____

_____

_____

_____

# Actions I Will Take:

_____

_____

_____

_____

**"Impulsive decisions based on emotional responses are often not the right decision."**

Jill J. Johnson

How can you ensure you don't make an impulsive decision?

_____

_____

_____

_____

_____

_____

_____

_____

_____

_____

_____

_____

_____

_____

## Actions I Will Take:

_____

_____

_____

_____

**"**When facing a tough decision be sure to get objective insight on the consequences of all your options.**"**

Jill J. Johnson

# Where can you obtain objective insight?

_____

_____

_____

_____

_____

_____

_____

_____

_____

_____

_____

_____

_____

# Actions I Will Take:

_____

_____

_____

_____

**66** *Good decision-making is a skill set that you develop and refine over time.* **99**

Jill J. Johnson

# How can you make better decisions?

_____
_____
_____
_____
_____
_____
_____
_____
_____
_____
_____
_____
_____
_____

# Actions I Will Take:

_____
_____
_____
_____

66 Don't allow yourself to be distracted by inconsequential decisions. Focus your decisions on things that matter. 99

Jill J. Johnson

# What do you need to focus on that matters the most to your decision?

_____

_____

_____

_____

_____

_____

_____

_____

_____

_____

_____

_____

_____

## Actions I Will Take:

_____

_____

_____

_____

**66**Having the right advisors can
be key when you are stuck on a
critical decision. This is when you
most need objective perspective.**99**

Jill J. Johnson

# Who can you reach out to, or hire, to assist with your decision?

_____

_____

_____

_____

_____

_____

_____

_____

_____

_____

_____

_____

_____

## Actions I Will Take:

_____

_____

_____

_____

**66**Understand all your options when you are making a hard decision. Consider options that make you feel uncomfortable.**99**

Jill J. Johnson

# Why do some of your decision options make you uncomfortable?

_____

_____

_____

_____

_____

_____

_____

_____

_____

_____

_____

_____

_____

_____

_____

# Actions I Will Take:

_____

_____

_____

_____

_____

**"**Evaluate all your decision options without drama and bias. They only convolute your evaluation of the options available to solve your problem.**"**

Jill J. Johnson

# How can you minimize drama and bias in your decision?

_____

_____

_____

_____

_____

_____

_____

_____

_____

_____

_____

_____

_____

_____

# Actions I Will Take:

_____

_____

_____

_____

_____

**"**Good decision assumptions are based on accurate information.**"**

Jill J. Johnson

How can you verify that the information you are using for your decision is accurate?

_____
_____
_____
_____
_____
_____
_____
_____
_____
_____
_____
_____
_____
_____

Actions I Will Take:

_____
_____
_____
_____

**"Even when things are at their darkest, you must trust yourself to find a way forward!"**

Jill J. Johnson

# What is something you can do to move forward?

---
---
---
---
---
---
---
---
---
---
---
---
---
---
---

## Actions I Will Take:

---
---
---
---
---

**"Knowing your boundaries for decision making will give you a more objective sense of how to evaluate your options."**

*Jill J. Johnson*

# What boundaries do you need to set for your decision?

_____

_____

_____

_____

_____

_____

_____

_____

_____

_____

_____

_____

_____

# Actions I Will Take:

_____

_____

_____

_____

**"Always take time to consider the potential unintended consequences of your decisions."**

Jill J. Johnson

# What are the potential consequences of your decision?

_____

_____

_____

_____

_____

_____

_____

_____

_____

_____

_____

_____

## Actions I Will Take:

_____

_____

_____

_____

**"To achieve success, you have to make bolder decisions!"**

Jill J. Johnson

# How can you be bolder?

_____

_____

_____

_____

_____

_____

_____

_____

_____

_____

_____

_____

_____

_____

_____

## Actions I Will Take:

_____

_____

_____

_____

_____

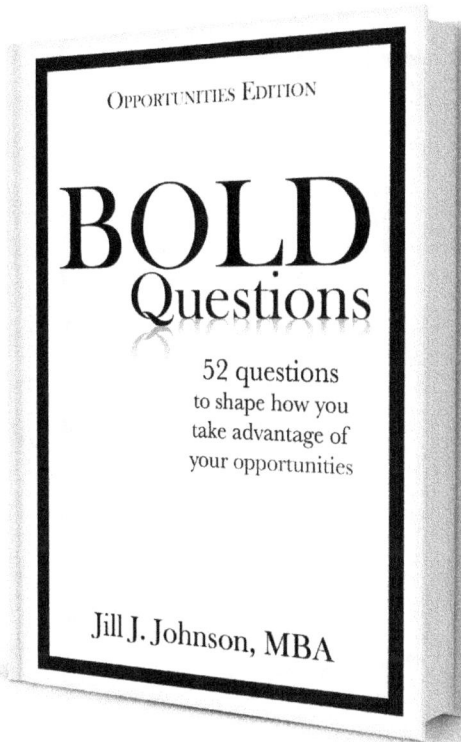